Big books

Big
books

December 1992
25

Dear Nicholas
Love
Grandma & Grandpa
Dalbis

DISCOVER

Communication

Educational Assessment Publishing Company, Inc.

San Diego

Note to the Family

The **DISCOVER** book *Communication* is organized around key concepts that are essential for helping children develop communication skills. Each page presents high interest, colorful illustrations that assist children in understanding the concept of communication. The content uses age-appropriate language that is necessary for young children to comprehend and retain the book's main ideas.

In addition to the colorful illustrations and the easy-to-understand language, a question introduces each key concept. The use of the question helps the child and the parent focus on the main idea. By reading the question, the parent can initiate a discussion to discover the child's understanding of a concept and to clarify family values before or after reading the pages to the child.

The early sections of the book describe and define the different types of communication. These parts of the book help children understand the concept. In the later sections of the book, children apply the concept to realistic situations to see how effective communication affects relationships. This strategy helps children and parents discuss communication in terms of the child's daily life.

Reviewers

The publisher wishes to thank the following reviewers of **DISCOVER** for their valuable comments. They provided specific comments on the content, organization, and difficulty level of the material. Their assistance has been invaluable in creating a book that will be usable and profitable for parents and children.

Susan A. Burgess, MAT
Consultant, Children's Literature
Westwood, MA

Bruce Frazee, Ed.D.
Associate Professor
Trinity University
San Antonio, TX

Eileen McWhirter McNabb
Former Region Administrator
Los Angeles Unified School District
Los Angeles, CA

Editorial, design, and production by Book Production Systems, Inc. Illustrations by Stephanie Pershing.

Copyright © 1990 by Educational Assessment Publishing Company, Inc.

All rights reserved. No part of this publication may be reproduced or transmitted in any form or by any means, electronic or mechanical, including photocopy, recording, or any information storage and retrieval system, without permission in writing from the publisher.

Requests for permission to make copies of any part of the work should be mailed to: Permissions, Educational Assessment Publishing Company, Inc., 1731 Kettner Boulevard, San Diego, CA 92101.

1 2 3 4 5 6 7 8 9 — 96 95 94 93 92 91 90 89   ISBN 0-942277-61-9

Table of Contents

Introduction

How do you tell someone what you are thinking? There are many ways to tell something. This is called communication. Communication is important because it helps people understand each other. Let's take a look at how to communicate.

What Is Communication?

Communication is sending and getting messages.
Think about talking with someone in your family.
You send messages by talking, and you get messages
by listening.

This happens whenever you talk with someone:
a friend, your teacher, or a neighbor. While you talk,
the other person listens. Then, when the other
person talks, you listen.

What Are Some Ways To Communicate?

There are many ways to communicate.
You can communicate by talking and listening.

You can communicate by sending and getting letters.

You can also communicate through body-language. Body-language is the way you sit or stand, the way your face looks, and how you hold your hands.

You can send messages about what you are saying
with your body.

You can send messages by smiling at people, and by looking at them when they are speaking.

You can send messages by walking straight and tall,
or by slumping your shoulders when you walk.

Why Is Communication Important?

Each person has a need for other people. Each person has a need to belong and to be loved.

Communication helps you get along with others.
It helps you feel that you belong.

What Are Good Ways To Communicate?

Communication is like a two-way street. People communicate best when messages, like cars, travel in both directions.

To be a good communicator, you need to send messages well and get messages well.

One way of telling your feelings can help people to really listen.

This is a way of saying what your feelings are. You can say, "I feel this way when you do that."

If you get messages well, you are a good listener.
A good listener learns more easily.

A good listener makes friends more easily. People like to be with a good listener.

To be a good listener, you need to show the other person that you are paying attention.

Look at the person, think about what the person is saying, and nod or ask questions to show that you are listening.

What Can Happen If Communication Is Not Good?

When communication between people is not good, people may not understand each other.

People may have arguments. People's feelings may get hurt.

How Can You Be A Good Communicator?

You can practice what you have learned. You can say, "I feel a certain way."

You can be a good listener.

Review

Now you know how to tell someone what you are feeling. Now you know how to listen better. Now you know that there are many ways of telling something. Communication is important. Now you know why. If you are a good communicator, you will be able to send and get messages better. This helps you to get along with others. And getting along with others will make you a happier person.

Note to the Family

The next two pages contain vocabulary and interactive activities that provide practice with the important words and ideas just learned. You can work with your child to reinforce these concepts.

Are You Puzzled by Communication?

Fill in the word puzzle.
Use the words from the
word bank to fill in
the blanks.

talking
messages
body-language
listener

DOWN

If you get messages well, you are a good _____.

You send messages by _____, and you get
messages by listening.

ACROSS

Communication is sending and getting _____.

_____ is the way you sit or stand, the way your face
looks, and how you hold your hands.

COMMUNICATION

Tic-Tac-Toe

Let's play tic-tac-toe!
Place an **O** in the squares
that are true. Place an **X**
in the squares that are
NOT true. Are you a
communication winner?

Communication is sending and getting messages.	Sending letters is the only way to communicate.	You can send messages using body-language.
Smiling at people is a way to communicate.	Each person has a need to belong.	Communication is like a one-way street.
A good listener learns more easily.	Asking questions helps to show that you are listening.	Good communication between people is not important.